How We Made It Over

ANDREA FREEMAN
CHANTELLE COLEMAN
ELLEN JOHNSON
SHANNON DAWKINS
ROBIN WORRELL-THORNE

1

ISBN: 978-0-692-26259-7 Published in U.S. by Changing Lives And Sincerely Supporting You, Inc.

Contents

Acknowledgements:

First, we would like to give thanks and honor to God who is the head of our lives. Secondly, we would like to thank every family member and friend who supported us throughout this journey.

1 *The Truth Revealed*
Author Robin Worrell-Thorne

Prelude-

It's not easy revealing a hidden truth and it's usually something that we hold on to for various reasons, out of fear of judgment, insecurity, rejection, or embarrassment. The truth will begin to consume us from the inside out if it is not released. My truth in various situations was painful to me, so I decided to guard it as much as I could. I would put on a facade and try to mask how I felt inside; but when I was alone, it would only hurt more. If telling my truth can relieve another of that painful feeling, then it's well worth telling to the world. In this chapter I will reveal the hidden experiences that I've overcome and expose to the reader how I made it over.

I was always raised to know God and to respect His place in my life. Unfortunately, I had to grow and learn —"the hard way"— how to have a relationship with Him. God was a — "place"— I would run to in times of trouble. Yes, I said He was a place to me and it hurts now to think of how I labeled God in my life. I had accepted Him in my heart as my savior, I believe that He died on the cross for my sins, and I even believe that He is coming back for those who have received Him, and are saved. My biggest setback, however, was the fact that my relationship with God was not personal. I did not consider Him as — "Daddy".— I came to realize through trial and tribulation in my life that He is not some secret place but He is a true miracle worker and He is alive today. I had to move Him from my head and place Him in my heart! My story is therapy for me but, hopefully, it will be an emotional help for those who are experiencing some of the same trials that I have gone through. I had to truly understand in my heart that trials surely come to make us strong.

It began with an abusive relationship, and then I was raped, next I watched my husband and both of my parents be buried, and I've been through cancer. Today, I count it all as part of — "The Plan"— for my life. I believe God has a plan for all of us. I also believe that if we put our Trust in Him and communicate with Him through prayer, He will allow us to walk through this life with the true comfort of knowing how to gain strength through our trials. I've learned that I need to tell my problems about my God, instead of telling my God about my problems. In EVERYTHING, I have to believe that The Father will make a way. This is not easy at all but, it is definitely worth it. In order to get to the truth, we must be honest with ourselves.

Abusive Relationship-

I spent many years loving a man so much that I honestly put him before everything. I believe that if Jesus himself had come and said, "Leave this man," I would have turned my back on Jesus and stayed in the relationship. I was very young and he was (what I considered) the love of my life. When I look back on this, I can honestly say, I needed to go through that situation to get to where I am today. Not that it was right, nor did I deserve to be abused. However, I have a stubborn spirit which would not submit to anything but my own personal feelings.

We often make the mistake of blaming others for what we go through, but we need to understand that some situations are allowed as part of our lives to make us stronger, or to help another. It's up to us and our Will to make the choice to press on and move past the tough times. I should have walked away from the abuse but I didn't until it showed up with full force. That was when I decided that I needed to pray for help to give me the desire to get away.

It was 25 years ago and I am certain that The Lord didn't allow me to live through this for nothing. God would want me to share and show others that we must make better choices and consult Him for answers. Abuse is never ok!

He was a very smart man and he was also — "street wise".— I was impressed by his willingness to protect me. He wasn't afraid to put his life in danger, to save mine. He knew a lot about life and he only told me what he wanted me to know. He was respected in the neighborhood and he made a name for himself. He was handsome and resourceful. He was a leader in his— "hood".— I was his prize possession (key word "possession"); but I was also very independent on my own. He wanted me to be more submissive and not have an opinion that differed from his. He would often remind me of all he did for me and how he would never allow me to leave him. Although there were many signs, I never thought he would physically hurt me.

It was a Friday evening and he came to my mom's house where he often would just walk in without knocking. Mom loved him and it was almost like he lived there. As he walked up the stairs, he was asking if I was ready to go with him to visit his grandmother. I had decided I didn't want to go but he could go without me. We had a son together and our son was two years old. I was ok with him taking our son for a visit to see his grandmother but I did not care to join them on this particular day.

He seemed upset because I did not want to go. It was shocking to find out how upset he really was. The disagreement quickly transpired into a fully-fledged argument. As the argument escalated he decided to push me into the bedroom wall. I proceeded with an instant instinct to defend myself; he stopped me in my tracks and hit me with a closed fist in my face! I did not believe this had happened, and as my mouth began to bleed; he went fleeing down the stairs and out the front door. I began to cry and went into the bathroom. I realized that I could not close my mouth without suffering excruciating pain!

My mother and son had already left the house before the altercation began. They were at the corner store. When they returned, I was sitting on the living room sofa in the worst pain I had ever experienced. My mom asked no questions. I just heard her calling my father on the phone saying, "This child needs to go to the hospital." When Dad pulled up in front of the door, he looked furious. I was so afraid that he was angry with me for being so stupid to allow this to happen. I thought it was my fault. The car was quiet on the 15 minute drive to the hospital. My mom was visibly shaken. My son was just looking at me and he kept saying, "Mommy's mouth is hurting." My Dad appeared very angry but wouldn't say a word.

We arrived at the hospital emergency room where my Mom and I were immediately told that I had a broken jaw and I would need surgery to reset the jawbone. I was devastated! A day later, I was barely able to speak with the hospital social worker who insisted I press charges against my attacker. I told her that I did not want to get him in any criminal trouble because he did not mean to hurt me. I explained that it was my son's father and I needed him in my son's life. I kept thinking, *"I love this man and things could change."* It didn't take long for me to realize love shouldn't feel like this and I should not be afraid of the man I love.

I prayed and asked God to help me to get over him. A few days later, I was greeted at home with flowers and a long apology letter. I eventually forgave him, but I never forgot what happened. We didn't continue our relationship. My parents were supportive in helping me with my son because I was not to see his father any longer. His father eventually went to jail and when he got out, he did not seem very interested in seeing our son, if he could not be in a relationship with me. My son and I moved on without him.

This situation haunted me for years, so much that I was reluctant to ever allow myself to get into another relationship. I needed to do some serious soul searching and ask God why this had happened to me and how I could go on. He slowly began to show me that I am not what I've been through. It took quite a few years but eventually I was able to move forward. I never looked back. I refused to. I know it was not by my own strength but it was surely my faith that helped me through.

Rape-

It was fall 1993 and my son was now six years old. We had been in our new apartment for about two years. It was a beautiful place and much cheaper than the place we had moved from. The neighbors seemed nice and since I worked two jobs, I would leave early and come home late. On this particular evening, after working from 9am to 11pm, I picked my son up from my sister's house and we went home to our apartment. It was very late, so my son and I went straight to our bedrooms and off to sleep. It didn't feel like I was asleep for very long when I was awakened by a strange man standing over me with a knife at my throat. He demanded that I pull the sheet over my face or he would go into my son's room and hurt him. Thankfully, my son slept through the entire assault, as the stranger proceeded to rape me at knife point.

"Where is God and how could He allow this to happen to me?" was all I could think. Do you not know that God allowed me to keep my sanity through the entire ordeal? I thought I would lose my mind but in the midst of it all I was silently praying that I would live through this horrendous ordeal and not contract any disease. Most importantly, I prayed with all of my heart that this person would not do anything to harm my son who was in the next room. Praise God for answering each one of those silent prayers!

The man continued and finished his business; and as he was leaving, he said that if I called the police, he would know and he would come back and hurt my son. I lay there in my bed for what seemed like an eternity before I got up and went into my son's room to check on him. I was afraid to move. I was afraid of what I would see in my son's room. I was afraid that the man would still be in the house. It was very dark and I moved quietly. When I entered my son's room, I found him sound asleep. He had not been touched. I began to thank God for His mercy! Thank you Jesus, for saving my baby and protecting him when I was unable!

The apartment was completely quiet as I walked into the kitchen. I noticed the butcher's knife had been removed from the — "knife block"— and the telephone was unplugged. I was trembling as I plugged the telephone back into the phone jack. All I could think of was to call my dad. I called him and begin to cry, as I stuttered the news that I had been sexually assaulted. I could tell that Daddy was trying to get himself together as if it were a bad dream. He asked if the person was still there and if I recognized him. Then he asked for my son. I told him I was really afraid and I had not called the police. Dad hung up immediately! I then called my sister and when her husband answered, all I could do was cry and mumble. He said they were on their way.

I stood in the kitchen for a moment and then went back into my son's room. I sat at the foot of my son's bed. He was still asleep. Suddenly, I heard a thunderous knock at the door that startled me and woke up my son. Dad yelled, "Open the door!" When I opened the door, it was my Dad with three police officers. They proceeded to ask questions and, in between the answers, I continued to ask if I could take a shower. The officers were very understanding but said that I would need to go to the hospital first and that I could take a shower after being seen by the doctors. I continued to speak with the officers while my dad looked on in total disappointment. He appeared to be very angry and one of the officers assured him they would look for the assailant. When my sister and brother in-law arrived they went into my son's room and took him out to their car. I was escorted to the police cruiser to be transported to the hospital. My dad followed along in his car and my sister rode with me in the police car.

At the hospital, I was asked to put all of my night clothes in a bag as well as my underwear. I was given a change of clothes to put on and the hospital detective said I would not be getting my night clothes back. He stated that they needed to take the clothes to the police station. It all seemed like an awful, disgusting nightmare, but it was very real! The nurse explained that I would be given, what they called, "a rape kit," and I was asked to urinate in a cup. They examined me and it seemed as if I was being violated all over again. I was very scared and really nervous.

I recall a lady talking me through all the tests and assessments that were taking place. She gave me several numbers to call within the next week. The numbers were for test results, rape victim counseling, and the police department. I was released from the hospital the next morning and my dad took me straight to my mom. Mommy looked so worried and told me to go in her room and just lay down. I never returned to my apartment.

The next several months were difficult. I was afraid to call out from work, because I did not want my managers to question why, so I continued working. I was very depressed. My entire attitude was different. I was extremely paranoid. I was reluctant to talk to my co-workers. I was not myself at all. I became over protective of my son and I was really edgy. I could sense that my mom didn't know what to say to me, so she would just do whatever she could to help ensure my son was taken care of. It seemed as if she was trying to alleviate me of any and all stress. My dad seemed like he didn't have the right words to say to me either, and it was hard for us to communicate like we used to.

After being with my mom for two months, I finally decided to try living alone again. I called the apartment and explained that I would be getting my furniture out and I made an appointment with the apartment manager to explain why I needed to break the lease. Due to the circumstances, the apartment manager seemed to understand. I was able to move into a new townhome on the other side of town. I settled there with my son and life slowly began to feel normal. I was hesitant about seriously dating anyone but I was also afraid to be alone. I spent time working and doing fun activities with my son. I visited my mom's house frequently and my sisters would be there. You could tell the rape had become a family secret that no one wanted to talk about. To my knowledge, the incident remains an open case; the rapist was never caught.

Husband-

Several years had passed and life for my son and I was beginning to have some sense of normalcy. My son was entering his last year of elementary school, and I had saved enough money to attend college. My sister continued to assist me with taking care of my son in the evening and I was able to work my full time job and attend school at night. My life became a daily routine and I had no time for a social life. I spent my weekends studying and spending time with my son. My son and I would discuss our week as we drove across town to visit my parents.

One Saturday afternoon I pulled up in front of my mom's house, and my sister was outside talking to her friend at his car window. My son ran over to say hello and I waved as I went into the house. My mom was in the kitchen cooking something delicious, as always. She hugged me and asked for my son. I went to the door to tell my son to come in and give his grandma a kiss, and I noticed a handsome young man with very nice dimples, outside with my sister and her friend. My son and I went back into the house and later my sister came in and said that the guy outside was her friend's cousin, and he wanted to meet me. Reluctant and hesitant, I went out and we were introduced. He was quite excited to meet me and we talked for what seemed like hours. We exchanged numbers and began calling each other daily.

It wasn't until a month or so later, that he asked to take my son and me out on a date. I accepted and we went to see a —"kid friendly"— movie, then out to dinner. I thought it was nice that he included my son on our date. We had a fantastic time! We began to see each other every weekend and I met his son as well. He would often visit my house along with his son, who was 3 years younger than mine. The boys got along well and things were beginning to get serious with me and my new boyfriend.

I met and spent time with his family, and he spent time with mine. My parents adored him and his family took an incredible liking to my son and me. Before long, he asked me to marry him and before I accepted, I thought it would only be fair to share my horrific experience with him. I explained that I had been raped years prior and I had not been sexually active since it happened. He was very understanding and said that he believed God sent him to me! He expressed some things he had gone through in his first marriage and was sure that we needed each other.

I prayed and asked God to help me in making my decision to spend my life with this man. It was clear that he was the man for me. Therefore, we became engaged. We spent every spare moment we could together. He was a truck driver and I was a supervisor in the medical lab. I was also attending school, so we made time to be together and did things with the boys almost every weekend.

It wasn't long before we were married. We purchased a starter home and we spent a great deal of time being a family who enjoyed each other and enjoyed life. What was dead inside me sexually was awoken again, by my husband. I felt whole. I enjoyed being a wife and mother of — "two"— sons. It was a good life.

During this time, my mom had two life threatening aneurisms and we had no other choice but to move her from her home to a nursing home for severe dementia. My husband was there for me through this and he visited my mother often, with or without me. He was a good man! We were good together and our good days outweighed any bad days.

My husband suffered from a heart condition that I didn't know about until a year before The Lord called him home. He left this earth suddenly on a hot August afternoon. He died at home and I felt like I died with him. I looked to my family for comfort but it was not easy. It was devastating for the boys as well. They were young men now, one in 11th grade and the other in his first year of college. We couldn't believe that God would come for my husband at the age of 38. In our eyes, my husband had so much more to accomplish and we felt his purpose had not yet been fulfilled. He loved everyone and everything. He was feisty and he enjoyed living his life.

I was a daddy's girl and ran to my father for comfort. I was upset with my spiritual father for calling my husband home at such a young age. I grieved for 5 years! Today, I realize that God makes no mistakes and there is a time and season for everything. My husband's journey was over and his assignment had been fulfilled. I miss my husband but I am trusting God's plan for me and I know in my heart that this was a scheduled event that God knew would happen. I am confident that

He will continue to see me through. Being a widow has made me a stronger and a better witness.

Mother and Father-

My parents were always great parents and very near and dear to each other. They spent time with us and taught us about life and life consequences through their actions. My parents were not strict but, each one had their own way of making us feel terrible if we disobeyed. Being the youngest, I felt the wrath of their discipline more than my siblings. It was always timely and I always learned the lesson the first time. Mom worried a lot and Dad didn't seem to worry about anything. They complimented each other so well. My parents were married for 58 years and today they are both with The Lord. I am sure of this because I was a witness when each one accepted Jesus as their personal savior.

My parents did so much together, even after they separated. It was no surprise that they were together when Mom fell to the floor at the bowling alley due to a massive aneurism. She spent several years in the nursing home after that tragic fall; but she was always surrounded by family. Dad visited daily, he loved my mom and his children so much. When Mom went to be with The Lord in 2011, it was very difficult but I understood her death better than when Dad went home in 2013. God has a plan for us all and we have to truly believe in our heart and soul that He makes no mistakes.

Dad was stricken with stage IV Cancer and passed away within a matter of 3 months. He was such a trooper to the very end and his only fight was him trying to show us that he was alright. The nurses would say he didn't want pain medicine during visiting hours because he didn't want us to see him drowsy and unaware. He was a very strong man! His death is so difficult to deal with, but my siblings and our children are left with wonderful memories. I know that God is still in control and my hope is built on nothing less than Jesus and His righteousness!

Cancer-

I was diagnosed with cancer and it has been a trying journey for me. My initial thought was "What else, Lord, and why me?" As I went through, I was thinking of my appearance more than how I felt. Vanity, maybe; however, my thought was if you look bad, you will begin to feel bad.

I also thought everyone around me who loved me would begin to feel sorry for me and treat me with a sympathetic tone. I wasn't ready for that! So I held it as long as I could from family, friends and coworkers.

I even left the church for a while but I never left God. I stayed away from family and friends. I even begin to treat the guy I had started seeing, differently, until he finally left me. It was a hard road because, in the back of my mind, I felt that I really didn't care if I lived or died. I felt I had no one and nothing left. It wasn't until I begin to talk about it with my sister and my close girlfriend that I began to heal. These two women each have a sincere spirit. They both know how to— "beat you until it feels better"!—

My sister will lay you out and feel sorry for you at the same time. I needed that more than anything. I love all of my sisters but there is a certain spirit in my second oldest sister that is so real and so valuable that I am blessed by her in so many ways. My sister is strong when she needs to be and weak when she has to be. She is my guardian angel and my life savior in so many ways.

My girlfriend was not made aware of the cancer diagnosis, because I did not want to upset her with more of my disappointment. I realize she had her own situations to deal with in her personal life. However, she can always sense when something is wrong with me. She can read my text messages and God will show her what to do or say to me. She consoled me, even when she didn't know she was doing so! We live in close proximity of each other and instead of just popping up, she would simply drop a card, a gift, or an encouraging message in my mailbox and then text or call me just to say, "Check your mailbox." I thank God for our friendship and sisterhood. I know without a shadow of a doubt that The Lord sent her to me. There are too many coincidences that He has allowed to confirm that He has brought us together. I am blessed by God's heart that is within her.

Beginning to realize that I am already healed as long as I believe, allowed me to feel better and muster the courage and zeal to go on! My trials have increased my faith. Whatever I am presented with; I have to be confident that I will get through it. As of today, I am in full remission and I am feeling wonderful! Besides… What better joy to have than knowing without a shadow of a doubt that you will always have eternal life and after this life, your life will be more abundant? I am blessed to be walking in my healing and I take pride in telling others my story.

Revelation-

As I tell my truth and reveal what I've been through, my goal is to bless another who may feel trapped in life's circumstances. I would tell that person to always know that you were created with a purpose and you are gifted to gift others. Trials come to make us strong. If we get the lesson or help another through our trials, it's well worth it. My advice is to always use your gifts for good and be sure you know how to determine your gift from what you are good at. We can be good at something but it may not be our gift.

Pray and ask God to reveal His plan for your life and don't be afraid to walk in it. Pay attention to life and where it is leading you. Be smart about your decisions and do all things in love, not for gain. Thanks for allowing me to reveal my truth in this chapter. I am still a work in progress, but telling my story to this point is a release for me that may relieve another.

To God be the Glory for what He has done!

2 *Whoopins: Getting Closer to Wholeness*

Author Shannon M. Dawkins

My parents divorced when I was about eight years old. I blamed myself. I guess kids always do that when their parents split up. My younger brother and I went to live with my grandparents. They were AWESOME and spoiled us, like grandparents tend to do. However, there were rules and expectations: homework right after school, bedtime at 8pm (8:30 when there was a special program on that we just had to watch!), chores on the weekends, bible study and choir rehearsal on Saturday (as well as during the week for other activities), and church every Sunday. We were expected to get A's and B's on our report cards, to respect all adults, love God and others as God loved us, and to treat others the way we wanted to be treated.

My grandparents were very calm people. There was no yelling or screaming in their house. Mom-Mom believed such behavior was uncivilized and disrespectful. My grandmother worked and my grandfather was retired. He made us breakfast in the morning, took us to school each day, and picked us up. He made sure that dinner was cooked every evening when Mom-Mom got home and we ate dinner together every evening at 5 o'clock. Sometimes during the week my mom would come to the house to visit. She would eat dinner with us and we'd be happy to see her, especially my younger brother. He missed her very much.

Weekends were the time Mom-Mom cooked. She always made a big breakfast. My favorites were her chipped beef on toast and corned beef hash. Talk about something delish! Even now, whenever I eat either of these dishes (which isn't often), I think of her. Mom-Mom also baked on the weekends: biscuits, cookies, lemon meringue pie, and homemade candy.

Some Saturdays I would help her sew. I'd help her pin the pattern on the fabric or cut the pieces of fabric out. I'd watch her sew the pieces together and stare in amazement when a finished product would emerge!

Saturdays were chore time. Even though I dried the dishes after dinner during the week, there were household chores that we did as a family. After breakfast, my brother and I each went to our room and cleaned it up. I would change my linen and his, while he helped Mom-Mom sort the laundry. I loved folding the sheets with my Pop-Pop. He would always make sure we folded them like sheets on a hospital bed. He would make the siren sound of an ambulance horn and then we'd meet in the middle.

After chores, we would go to church for Bible Study and choir rehearsal— then it was off to Dairy Queen! Later that evening Mom-Mom would cook dinner for the next day. She did not believe in doing any chores whatsoever on Sunday, it was the Lords day. Sundays were reserved for church. Morning service followed by an afternoon service, if there was one. If not, we would have a family dinner with my mom and other relatives who would stop by. We would relax, take a nap after dinner, watch TV, and spend time as a family together.

My grandparents were amazing people to me. They took us in, cared for us, nurtured us, loved us—wholly, completely, totally and unconditionally. They made us feel safe and wanted. They took us on vacation, taught us right from wrong, to love God, how to order from an adult menu, the type of service to expect when you're spending your money, and other life lessons I still remember and use to this very day.

Pop-Pop used to take us to Jamaica Queens to see his favorite brother, Uncle Herb, who had grandkids around my age. I loved going there, even though Uncle Herb never let us hang out in NY! Once, while we were there, I remember hearing Pop-Pop say, "It's not right, it's not right! They can't go!" Then Mom-Mom replied, "She's their mother, Youngie. They have to go." I saw my grandfather cry that day, something I had never, ever seen before. Somehow I knew that my life would never be the same. I was 12 years old, and found out that my brother and I were going to live with our Mom during summer vacation in Jamaica Queens.

My brother was ecstatic about going to live with our mom. While he loved Mom-Mom and Pop-Pop to pieces, he was crazy about his momma! Whenever she would come to my grandparents' house for dinner or to visit, he was always hugging her, tugging at her, and trying to get her attention when she was talking. Me? I loved my mom, but I wanted to stay with my grandparents. I didn't feel as connected to her as I did to my grandparents. I didn't know why that was. I just knew I felt that way.

Life at my mother's was somewhat the same. We still had expectations and rules: get good grades, do our homework right after school, do our chores, respect all adults, and go to church. However, we now had to take the bus to school and come home to an empty house afterwards. My grandparents did not like that (and neither did I)! Since I was the oldest, I was responsible. I had to make sure that I had my key to get in; I answered the phone when mom called, we changed out of our uniforms, me and my brother's homework was done before she got home from work. When my mom got home, she made dinner and we ate together as a family.

On Saturdays, we did our chores, went to bible study and choir rehearsal. Afterwards, we would go to the movies or do some other fun thing. We used to love going to the store to pick out records. We loved music! We always had the latest records and albums. On Sundays we went to church and then over to my grandparents' house for dinner. I loved going over there! I never wanted to leave. My favorite weekends were when we were able to spend the whole weekend at my grandparents'. Pop-Pop would pick us up on Friday evening and he'd take us home after Sunday dinner.

Yes, life for us at my mom's was similar to living with my grandparents. However, we were living with a dark and ugly secret, experiencing something foreign to us that we had never experienced before. We were physically and emotionally abused by my mother. It took me years to say those words and even longer to fully acknowledge their impact. I didn't realize at the time that we were being abused. I just knew that something wasn't right about it.

Back in the 70's, lots of my friends got spankings as a punishment. It's just the way it was back then. We also knew that the bible said, "Spare the rod, and spoil the child." We even got spanked once by our grandparents after we broke the kitchen table playing Twister on it. Yes, we played Twister, on top of my grandmother's yellow Formica table! Pop-Pop spanked my brother and Mom-Mom spanked me, with a folded up section of the newspaper. Can you believe that? Boy did we cry like the world was over? I mean water works! But that spanking was nothing compared to the whoopins we got at my mom's.

When I say whoopins— that's exactly what I mean. I got beat with belts, hairbrushes, the iron cord, the extension cord, whatever my mom had handy. What did I get a whoopin for? Anything! If my neighbor saw me doing something wrong, I got a whoopin. If my teacher said I was acting up or talking in class, I got a whoopin. If my brother did something he wasn't supposed to do, I got a whoopin, because I was the oldest and thus responsible for him. If my mom thought I had done or said something, or even looked a certain way, I got a whoopin. So, guess what? I got LOTS of whoopins! Not only did I get whoopins, I got slapped, punched, and had stuff thrown at me. I didn't know a shoe could be used like a boomerang until my mother threw one at me.

I definitely can't forget being cussed out. Chile, please! My Mother cussed me out so much that I grew up thinking my name was "Bitch". There were many days that I went to school with whelps, bruises, a fat lip and a crushed spirit.

I loved my mother, yet I was confused and angry. Is this how a mother is supposed to talk to and treat her kids? I didn't think so. Mom-Mom never treated us like that. I wondered what my brother and I did that was SO bad to deserve getting beat and talked to like we were nothing. Were we — "perfect kids"—? Of course we weren't, however we weren't rude, ill-behaved, disrespectful, unruly hellions either. I just could not understand why she didn't just leave us at our grandparents' house. I figured we were the same kids that we were with them and they never beat us and talked to us like my mom did. When did we become so horrible?

At first I used to tell my grandfather about it. My brother never wanted me to. He used to say, "Shannon, don't say anything! You're really gonna get it! Don't say anything!!" I didn't listen though and I told. I knew Pop-Pop said something to her, because she'd throw it up in my face. She would scream in my face, "Bitch, you think your precious grandfather can save you? He can't stop me! I'm YOUR MOTHER! I can do what I want. I brought you in this world and I'll take you out!" Then she'd go right back to the same ole, same ole.

I stopped telling my grandfather. I don't know why I did, I just did. Somehow I knew this was my lot in life, and I just accepted it as it was. There was nothing he could do, I thought. There was nothing the police could do either. My mom used to tell me, "You can call the cops if you want to. They betta keep your ass, cause when they return you to me, I'm really gonna beat the shit out you!" Needless to say, I never called them. So, I just dealt with it.

I read books, lots of books, dreaming about a better life. My mom got mad at that, and called me "bougie" and stuck up. She said I needed to get my head out of the clouds and live in the real world. She would yell, "You ain't gonna live like them people in those books. Stop dreaming! That's your problem, you think you better than everybody! You ain't better; you ain't shit— just like your trifling ass Daddy!"

I would keep on reading though, dreaming of living a different life. I'd live in a beautiful place with lots of sun and blue water. A place that was peaceful and calm, where people got along and treated each other well. I dreamed of being a successful pediatrician, living in a huge house with a great husband and children who we loved and cared for. I dreamed of the day I could get out! I prayed too, a LOT! I prayed to God every night, asking Him to save me and my brother from this house. I asked Him why we had to live like this. What had we done to deserve this? Why couldn't we go back to Mom-Mom and Pop-Pop's? I didn't understand. Were we evil? Were we awful children? He never answered my prayer though. He never saved us. So, there it was. No relief for us. God had forgotten about us. I didn't want to believe it.

We learned in church that God always took care of His children. That He always made a way for them. I had heard our pastor tell the story of the Israelites who were enslaved for years, abused and mistreated, then God sent Moses to rescue them and their tormentors drowned in the Red Sea. I figured if I was good, God would send someone to rescue us.

I was the oldest so it was my responsibility to save my brother. I studied harder and even got better grades. I made sure my brother's homework was completed properly. I cleaned the house and helped my brother with his chores. I went to church, sang in the choir, went to bible study and read my Bible. I memorized scripture and could hold my own in a conversation about God with grown-ups. I just knew that God was pleased and would send a rescuer. He didn't.

I was mad at God. I knew it was a sin to be mad at God, but I was. I could not believe that He allowed us to be taken from our Grandparents to live with a mother who I thought was crazy. She was so nice to us one minute— taking us out, buying us stuff, laughing, joking and having fun— then the next minute we're getting called names, slapped, and punched. I just didn't get it.

I remember one Sunday in church, the choir sang "God Will Open Doors For You". As I sat there next to my grandfather, I whispered to him, "I wish God would open a door for me and my brother." He said to me, "Peach, He will. Just keep praying and believing that He will, and He will." I couldn't see it though. I wanted to believe Pop-Pop because he never lied to me. He and Mom-Mom were people of great faith and I wanted to be like them. So I held on and kept praying, waiting for the door to open for me and my brother.

God never sent a rescuer or opened a door for us. Therefore, I continued to work on my own way out—college! I could not wait to get to college, somewhere far, far away from home. I didn't want to leave my grandparents and I certainly didn't want to leave my brother. He'd be all alone with her, with no one to look out for him. That made me so sad. Yet, I had to go. I had to be free. I wished I could have taken him with me.

During my years as a college undergrad, I did my best to enjoy life. I partied, pranked the girls on my floor, went to class, changed my major from biology to health administration (organic chemistry and I were NOT friends!) and became a student leader on campus. I helped organize rallies and protests against apartheid (did I mention I'm a bit of a revolutionary?), made new friends, played in all night pinochle sessions, pulled all-nighters, and did I say partied? I thoroughly and completely enjoyed my college experience. Attending a predominately white institution, there was always a Frat party. I used to invite my brother up to campus so he could see that college was truly an escape.

I still prayed, although it was mostly for my grandparents and my brother. I didn't ask God for much when it came to me anymore. I figured He didn't care about me because if He did, He would have stopped those whoopins I got. He would have saved me from being called out my name all the time and being talked to like a dog. But He didn't. He allowed us to stay there and be abused. I had gotten out on my own and all I wanted Him to do was protect my little brother. That's it. I was in college now, so I was good.

After college, Pop-Pop wanted me to come home and stay home. He never wanted me to go away in the first place. He couldn't understand why I didn't want to go to Temple and live on campus. I told him I applied for Temple's MBA/JD program but couldn't go until May (I graduated in December), and of course my mother was her usual self. "Bitch, you getting the hell outta here! You ain't staying here! You betta go on down to Maryland with your brother," she yelled.

That was exactly what I did. I started grad school in Maryland, that coming January. In grad school I was able to look after my brother. We were together again! I was so happy he was free too. He had a girlfriend who he wanted to marry, and he did marry her. I was happy he had someone else to love him. I prayed that God would bless him with a wonderful, loving wife, someone who was kind and gentle, who would love him as I loved him and treat him like he was the most special person on Earth. I prayed that she'd be someone who would always be there for him and never leave him, like I had. I still felt guilty for leaving my baby brother alone with my Mother to fend for himself. He found that in his wife and I was grateful. Finally, God had answered one of my prayers.

After grad school the plan was to work in downtown Philly and live in Rittenhouse Square.

Of course my mother had commentary. "You's a Bougie Bitch, always have been! What makes you think you can live in Rittenhouse Square?" I don't know why I expected her to support my plan, when she never fully supported any of my dreams: going to Howard, being a pediatrician, or pledging a sorority. On the surface she would fake it, yet she'd always down me for having big dreams; always had negative commentary about them. Needless to say, those plans didn't work out (surprise, surprise) and I had to live with mother— again. Nine months of misery, until I decided to move back to Maryland.

Living in Maryland was great. I didn't have to hear the negativity every day. Yet talking to my Mother was hit or miss. Most times, the conversation ended with yelling, screaming, cursing me out and her slamming down the phone. There was always something with her. She didn't like my brother's wife, so I shouldn't; she didn't know why I wouldn't come home, or if I did why I only visited Mom-Mom. She couldn't understand when she called my office (10 times a day), why she couldn't get straight through to me. Talk about frustrating! I tried to be the adult and talk with her rationally; it didn't work. She never listened; just yelled, screamed, hollered and cursed. No matter the situation, it was always my fault. I was always the — "bad guy"—, and she was always the victim. If something happened to me at work, it was because I was a bougie, snobby bitch. If I had a bad day, it was because I was a nasty, evil bitch. If I didn't feel like talking to her, I was an ungrateful and disrespectful bitch. Trying to get through to a person who chooses not to listen to you when you are trying to explain how their words hurt is exhausting and a waste of time. Therefore, I stopped and did me.

What do you think happens to a girl child who is repeatedly called a "B" by her own mother? Who is told, by her mother, that she "ain't shit"? Who is beaten, smacked, punched and slapped - for any minor infraction? What do you think happens to her self-esteem, her self-image, her self-worth, her confidence? She crumbles inside — that's what. She grows up not loving and valuing herself. She becomes hollow, empty, and broken. She allows people, places and things into her life that shouldn't be and it takes a long time, a lot of hard work and prayer to undo the damage.

I did me, and I did me well. I was in the hair salon every other week getting my "do did." I shopped till I dropped buying the latest clothes and shoes. I hit the nail salon every other week getting fresh designs. Hunnties, I was CA-UTE! And I hung out—dinner, movies, concerts, and parties. If there was a hot party, I was there, drinking, smoking cigarettes, and getting my groove ALL the way on! Men? Of course Chile! I had a dollar and several pieces of change! I had it going on.

I thought my life was great: I had my own apartment, fly clothes, shoes, friends, lots of suitors, and a great job. I could do whatever I wanted, when I wanted, with whom I wanted and no one could tell me anything! I was in control of MY life. I stopped going to church and reading my Word on a regular basis. I thought to myself, *"What for?" God answered my prayers for my brother and I am good.* I never prayed for anything significant for myself anymore anyway. Even though deep down in my soul I wanted to be a mother and a wife, I didn't allow myself to pray for those things. Instead I chose to be a rebel, a young, free spirited, upwardly mobile, educated woman.

I dated men who weren't worthy of me. I felt like, "I ain't gonna marry none of these dudes, so whatever, who cares?" I dated a hustler who worked full-time and slung on the side. He was a cutie, and looked like the R & B singer Joe. He had a son and a girlfriend. Next! I dated a chef who looked like the rapper Method Man. He lived with his ill mother, brought me nice gifts, and wound up in the hospital (they called me while I was shopping). He had overdosed on morphine and they brought him back. Next! Then there was the up-and-coming artist. He didn't have a job, because he was working on his — "art"—. Next! Then there was the Army dude. He was actually a decent, good guy. He was so sweet and treated me well. Problem? He was TOO nice (I know - that's SO dumb! I was young and didn't know any better). I talked to him like crap, and he never said a word, he just let me. What a whuss! Next!

I met —"him"— on a gorgeous spring day. He rolled down the street in a gold Acura with the window down. He drove past me, stopped the car and said, "Hello, how are you, beautiful?"

"Fine, thank you," I replied, as I continued to walk down the block toward home.

He drove slowly down the street beside me and said, "You look nice today. Do you have a friend?"

I politely said, "Thank you and no."

"Do you want one?" he asked.

I answered, "Maybe." He then stopped the car and I was able to get a good look at him. He had almond brown-skin, dazzling, perfect white teeth, and was fine! He looked like the lead singer of the 90's group H-Town. We exchanged numbers, and it began.

He was a high school football star, ex-military grocery store manager who grew up with means. He went to private school, grew up skiing and vacationed all over the United States. After one semester of college in the ATL, he came back to Maryland. His parents were divorced, he was raised by his grandmother, and he was an addict. I didn't know he was an addict when I met him, I found out much later. By then, it was too late. I was hooked.

Before meeting him, I had gone back to church and rededicated my life to the Lord. I had made my — "List"—, prayed over it and placed it in the Bible. I was attending church and bible study regularly, and was also active in several ministries. After meeting him, I thought, *"Is God finally sending me 'The One'?"* —"The One"— I hoped for deep in my soul but was too afraid to pray for; —"The

One"— who would heal my brokenness; —"The One"— who would love me completely, totally and unconditionally. WAY too much pressure on one person, right?

All was good, so I thought. Even though I let him move in (wrong!), even though we were being intimate (dead wrong!) and my beloved brother had told me he thought —"The One"— was using drugs (dead and stanking wrong!), I justified it by saying, "That was his past, I am his future. We worship together; he's changed. We're going to get married and have a family. He's The One." Wrong, Wrong, Wrong, WRONG!

One night, the Lord came to me and I heard Him, clear as a bell in the dead of night, say to me, "You are sleeping with evil." I woke up and fell to my knees, shaking and crying. —"The One"— woke up and asked me what was wrong. I told him I could feel evil. He got down on his knees with me and began to pray with me. Crazy, right? I heard straight from the Lord's mouth that I was in a HOTT mess, and instead of running in the opposite direction, I continued to justify my mess.

It would take an entire book to chronicle the madness that was our —"relationship"—. What I will say is that it left me more broken than I ever was before him. Every fear, every scar, every insecurity, every pain that lived inside of me reared its ugly head. It strained my relationships with the people I cared most about in this world. It brought me face to face with the ugliness of abuse and the scars within that I never took the time to heal. It brought me face-to-face with why: Why would you allow that? Why would you choose that? Why would you stay and accept that? It brought me to my knees, crying out to The True ONE who loved me from the start; who had been waiting to heal my brokenness; who loved me wholly, completely, totally and unconditionally; who had been with me all along. It wasn't until I was so low, so tired, and I had been so whooped by my choices, that I had no choice but to run back to the God I met as a child.

When I walked away from that —"relationship"—, I walked towards God, my Father and I never looked back. I was never was one to share all of myself with others, I only told parts of what was going on with me. One reason was, because I didn't want to be judged, and another reason was because I believed that if someone knew the full story, it made me vulnerable to being hurt to my core. I knew what that felt like from my mom and I was adamant that I would never let that happen to me again. I still struggle with that today. I have a hard time letting people all the way in. I'm working on it though!

With God, I didn't have to tell Him anything, He already knew my entire story, from soup to nuts. I had to re-learn what God says about me: that before He formed me in my Mother's womb, He knew me and had set me apart (Jeremiah 1:5). I had so much to forgive myself for and I wanted to, I just didn't know how. I had so much to heal from and I wanted to, I just didn't know how. However, what I did know is that I wanted to change. I wanted to heal and I wanted to be the best — "me"— I could for myself and my infant son.

I sought therapy to begin to deal with the depression that engulfed me; I wrote a journal to give voice to my unspoken experiences. I prayed and cried to God for release—release of pent-up anger, hostility, resentment, and self-hate—so that I could be free, truly free. Free to love myself, forgive my mother, and break the cycle of abuse for my son.

This process of achieving wholeness has not been easy, and yes, it is a process. I would be lying if I said that I never have self-doubt and insecurities, because I do. I would be lying if I said that I never have a day when those old feelings and thoughts creep back into my consciousness, because they do. What I will say instead is that today I have a choice! Each day the Lord allows me to see, I can either choose Christ's view of me, or I can continue to choose someone else's version of me. Every day that I choose Christ's view of me is another day I move closer to wholeness, for I am more than a conqueror in Jesus Christ who loves me (Romans 8:37).

I am still learning to forgive myself. This is a hard one because I'm very hard on myself. I'm working on it though. I have, however, forgiven my mother, as Christ forgave me (Ephesians 4:32, Matthew 6:14-15, 1 Peter 3:9). Forgiving her hasn't been easy because of the perpetual hurts she's inflicted over the years, even some most recently. I must forgive her because I will no longer allow someone else's issues to affect me or influence me, not anymore. At almost fifty years old (next month) I get to enjoy my life, and as my brilliant brother reminded me most recently, anyone who can't add value to my life has got to go!

I still grieve some days for that young girl, who only wanted to be loved and cared for by her mother. Some days when I speak, the words come out harsher than I intended them to and I am reminded of how my mother spoke to me. That lets me know I still have work to do. In those moments when I am tempted to down myself; in those moments when I don't feel pretty or valuable, or worthy of good things, I remind myself that God doesn't make junk!

I was created in the very image of God (Genesis 1:27). I remind myself that God has brought me from a mighty long way. I remind myself of what God says about me: that I am fearfully and wonderfully made (Psalm 139:14); that He loved me so much that He sent His only Son into the world to die for me (Romans 5:8, John 3:16); that He will heal my broken heart and my wounds (Psalm 147:3). Not only do I have to remind myself, I have to believe what my Father says about me, for God is not a man that He should lie (Numbers 23:19).

As I sit and look at my sleeping son, I cannot imagine calling him out of his name. I cannot imagine beating him until I am tired, covering his body with whelps. I cannot imagine saying or doing anything that would intentionally damage his self-esteem and self-worth. I am grateful that I was able to experience love from my grandparents and the love of God. Now, I am able to love myself. It is that love that allows me to love my son—wholly, completely, totally and unconditionally.

3 _From Beast to Beauty_

Author Ellen Johnson

Insecurity is that beast that comes into your life and shakes it to the core. It floods into your life that day when you learn that the sperm donor who helped to get you into this world wants nothing to do with you. It's that day when a young woman you poured into with your time, resources, and prayer admits that she has been sleeping with your man. It's the day when the company you have worked for more than 13 years with strong performance gives you a pink slip. Insecurity is the beast that slays you but spares your life. It knocks the wind out of you, leaving you with only enough breath to get to your knees and groan in short, desperate whispers, "God help me."

Insecurity took life form in my life at an early age when I found out the truth about the man who made the deposit that helped to get me into the Earth realm. The same man who stated he wanted nothing to do with me. I denied and lied to avoid accepting a truth that made me question my worth over my entire lifetime. It has been the root cause of my past use of alcohol and nicotine to try to fill voids and the emptiness I felt. Although that

51

beast, insecurity, dares me to take steps to rid myself of its hateful effects, I accept the challenge because of a promise God made to me back in 1996. "Be strong and courageous. Do not be afraid; do not be discouraged for the Lord your God will be with you wherever you go" (Joshua 1:9).

In my human frailty, with insecurity as its co-pilot, mistakes are shaped into calculated actions. It's when I am mentally, physically, and emotionally tired, beat down by the disappointments of life, that I barely know whether I'm coming or going. It's the decision to smoke that first cigarette as a teenager, dismissing the looming addiction factor that has been forecasted. It's the work required to forget what has hurt me. It's in the realization that perfection is unattainable. It's that beast called insecurity that causes fear to crouch at every door waiting to attack.

Conversely, my spiritual enablement teaches me the most valuable lessons from my mistakes and helps me make the necessary corrections. It gives sweet rest in the trust I have in the most-high source of power and authority over my life. It restores the decades lost battling with addiction and empowers me to make the ultimate decision to live a healthy, faithful, abundant life. It erases the hurt but promotes the lesson the hurt taught me. It demands me to strive for excellence as a much more satisfying and attainable goal.

Even in my spiritual growth, I continually live at the risk of my insecurities being triggered. Most of the time it's— "game on,"— and I don't let insecurity show out, but there's those times when I get a rush of unhealthy emotions, and good sense and sound thinking "Fly right out the window." No matter how big of a fool I make of myself on the outside with fits of rage, crying and shouting obscenities, I feel like a bigger one on the inside. Even worse is when I don't say a word, but my expressions give me away. I know that my reaction has an emotional implication, but an even greater spiritual one.

Knowing that I have the God-given right to live free, whole, and secure does not cancel the feeling that I have earned the right to be hurt, angry, and insecure. When painful memories of rejection, job loss, mistrust, and further being overly sensitive, misunderstood, and unappreciated surface, pride talks me out of forgiving her, or him, or them, and even myself. Sometimes pride drives me to destruction and distraction from what is best for me, even though I know forgiveness is not for them. I've been challenged with the question, "If you have forgiven, what gives me the right to talk about the offense?" Let me be clear, I am on a journey toward forgiveness. No one else has the right to decide the length or distance.

Insecurity can make a complete fool out of you if you let it. I can only thank and praise God that, when I came face-to-face with the so-called friend who violated my home and marriage, I chose to take the first step toward forgiveness by accepting the apology that was rendered. Trust me, I had many choice words in my head that I could have said, but God assured me that at the time of the Lord's vengeance, He will render unto her recompense. To add insult to injury, I had to face the reality that there are women in the church who are still running the devil's errands. They get a kick out of testing the fortitude of men, even married men. This is the most dangerous kind of insecure woman who is willing to play a part in the devil's scheme and destroy a marriage. Insecurity makes her do foolish things in order to feel better. Infidelity is one of these sneaky little devils that cause substantial hurt, limitations, and distractions to all parties involved and keeps each one from the effectiveness or fulfillment of purpose, and from the powerful and abundant life Jesus has promised. I had to pray and study, give and serve, and plead with God to help me find a way out of my own feelings of insecurity.

For me, insecurity is about losing my God given dignity. The enemy of my soul loves that and wants me to stay stuck in self-hatred. It's hard work to break this cycle, but the good news is that I am recognizing the triggers and intentionally responding to them differently. I have learned that the process of developing a belief system has to first make its way into my head on its route to my heart. I have decided that insecurity does not have the right to keep me from living free in Christ Jesus as He performs a miracle on my heart and my mind. I am reclaiming my God-given dignity.

The Word of God in Proverb 31:25 has promised to clothe me with strength and dignity. I have dignity because God gave it to me. God has it and He created me in His image. He crowned me with it. God-given honor and dignity was not just put in my hands, but He put it on my head. He wrapped it as a crown around my mind where it is something that I know I have, even when I don't feel it.

The month of March was a particularly eventful time. I received a phone call from the Women's Ministry Leader and, honestly, I cannot remember whether I was asked or told that I would participate, but it really doesn't matter because the Holy Spirit immediately said, "Your answer is yes." A few days after that phone call, I received an email with details and a list of suggested topics for the series, and again the Holy Spirit spoke so clearly to me and said, "Your topic is Insecurity," which was one of the topics listed in the email. Further, the Holy Spirit urged me to call the Women's Ministry Leader right away so that no one else would select that topic before me.

In the same month of March, my employer tasked me to participate on the proposal team to place a bid on the government contract that I had worked for the past six years. This task required me to work twelve- to fourteen-hour days, six to seven days a week for about six weeks straight, and at the end of all that, we lost the contract to the lowest bidder. It didn't seem to matter that we were the only ones technically qualified to do the work. Within a few days of the announcement that we had lost the contract, I found myself in the office with my Principal, Deputy Program

Manager, and Human Resources to share with me that my position with the firm would be terminated, or softly described as a lack of work letter. They were kind enough to give me 30 days to land a position; a severance pay in the world of contracting.

When my biggest fears were valid, and threats to my survival were real, and I was being swept away in a wave of insecurity, it took nothing less than the divine power and wisdom of God to give me the clarity of thought to keep me from losing my mental balance, going crazy and saying and doing things that I'd regret. This job loss dropped me into a pit of fear and unhealthy emotions. I had to get to my power source and ask myself, "Who and what am I afraid of and why am I afraid?" I refused to be jealous and self-loathing. All I could do was strive to look, act, and respond right, while the fear of being rejected, being betrayed, being insignificant, being hurt, and being disrespected swept over me in waves.

I am so glad that God is in the business of changing those of us who are brave enough and choose to enter into the process of change. I came to accept that the brick walls I was hitting were a change of direction. I agreed not to despise the trials of my faith. For the second time in my life the scriptural passage in the first chapter of the book of James came alive, the one that says, "...count it all joy when you fall into divers temptation." Believe me, I was tempted to say and do a lot of things, but I agreed to let my faith operate in patience and let patience have her perfect work that my response to all that was coming against me would be perfect and entire, according to the scripture; and I reaped the benefit of wanting for nothing. Of course, I was under close scrutiny for my emotions and reactions. So I knew I needed to react with a heightened sense of awareness and change the way I was feeling, thinking, and acting. I had to stop and remind myself that I am clothed in strength and dignity, and my goal is to be whole and free.

My emotions and responses don't always show up politely, but pretending like I have no reaction is not an option. I had to address offenses and set boundaries but refuse them the right to hold me hostage. I had to acknowledge being hurt, disappointed, shocked, unsure, and humbled without allowing these things to touch the deeper part of me or my sense of worth and value. I had to be willing to make the change for the legacy I'm passing on to my girl children and grandchildren. My choice is to live the abundant life that the Lord has set before me —full of love and purpose and security.

I can assure you that the culmination of activities in the month of March was a God idea because only He knew that I would be living through the second greatest affliction of my life. Talk about needing God to navigate me through the insecurity in my life.

Imagine the fear and insecurity that has set in one year later, still unemployed. Make no mistake, at times I've been a complete emotional mess. I am fragile, overly sensitive, and unable to look beyond my status, my inadequacies, or myself. However, through the haze of my pain, I'm finding the real me. I thought I was clear about me, but I'm discovering another level of me. It is that place in me where I can fully rest in the light of God's Love.

Through my pain, again I prayed and studied and gave and served and pleaded with God to help me understand all my feelings of insecurity. I learned that insecurity refers to a profound sense of self-doubt—a deep feeling of uncertainty about your basic worth and place in the world. Insecurity is linked with self-consciousness, a lack of confidence, and fear about your relationships. Well, well, well, now doesn't that describe my life? Here I am, uncertain whether my desires and feelings are legitimate. Here I am again in my life, living in the fear of rejection. I learned that insecurity is not just about a lack of security, it's also a lack of faith. I did not only doubt myself, I doubted God. Therein is my biggest problem. I can't possibly know myself better than the Creator and Master of the universe who called me out of darkness into His marvelous light. Even as flawed as I am, I am confident that He has called me and equipped me for work in His Kingdom. God uses people along the path to encourage you and remind you that He has not left you.

When life gives you lemons in the form of a job loss, what does a girl do? Well, you go get yourself some sugar and make lemonade, of course. You thank God for your grandmother who told you to put away a little something, a "rainy day" fund, to have in case "he" loses his mind and walks out on you. You know … just in case. Then there is the 401K fund that the government double dares you to touch so they can punish you with the ridiculous federal and state taxes you pay on all your earnings in this great United States of America. But that's alright, it was there. Rather than bitterness, I choose to live in the affirmation of the late, great Maya Angelou, whom I affectionately call "MA" that says, "I can be changed by what happens to me, but I refuse to be reduced by it."

Beauty began to form in my life the moment that I released my earthly father and accepted that my Heavenly Father will wrap me in His arms and love me with an everlasting love, love that is and does flow through my life like a river.

Beauty is that awesome day when I received a phone call from the Women's Ministry leader who asked me to be one of seven women selected to participate in a Summer Bible Study series, and I accepted the challenge to teach through my pain. I gave God my ashes. He fulfilled an opportunity to be used by Him in me.

Beauty was personified when I walked up into the face of the other woman, held her hand, and spoke the words, "I forgive you," and gave my broken heart to God to begin the long journey of repairing it. Beauty is when your children, husband, friends, and even associates call you blessed. Every time that beast, insecurity, shakes your life, slay it with beauty.

I wish you security.

4 *Loving Me From The Inside Out*

Author Chantelle Coleman

August 1, 2013 was the day that I decided to give love a chance. The day I decided to truly see the woman who had been staring back at me for 43yrs—a woman who remained hidden in darkness wearing a garment of depression; a woman in bondage, a slave to her own fears and insecurities. It was my faith and determination that pushed me forward to take that one step that would begin my journey, the one step in the direction of being renewed and the one step towards my journey of healing. It was that one step that I took towards the journey of "Loving Me from the Inside Out."

I think about all of the years I wasted on being afraid to live; all of the missed opportunities and the lost footage of my life. My pain started years ago. Being an only child, I spent a lot of my time alone while my mom worked hard to provide the best life for me that she possibly could. Even when I let her down, time after time, she was my biggest cheerleader and never stopped showing me unconditional love. Although my mom never withheld any opportunities from me, she never pushed me really hard and I took advantage of that.

My parents have always believed in me, and could see the great things that I could never see within myself.

Throughout my life I have clearly had some tragedies that I have kept hidden not just from my mom and my family but I also buried them in a dark place within myself. I didn't face those tragedies and that was the beginning of a cycle of keeping secrets. I didn't trust the people in my life to protect me and I allowed my pain, fears and tragedies to simmer and finally boil over into every aspect of my life. Molested numerous times at a young age, I lost me, I lost my voice and I lost my fight. I was the little girl who never shared her pain. Since the age of 11, I never went to amusement parks or rode rides. I was the little girl who dreaded going to school because I knew I would end up being the joke of the day. I knew that I would come home and instead of talking about my day I would eat away the pain. That was the beginning of me spiraling out of control.

I somehow always managed to go through life pretending I didn't have a care in the world. There was no urgency about anything for me. I didn't think about how I looked or being in style. I always settled for just getting by. I never tried to excel or draw attention to myself.

Shackled and bound, I sabotaged my own life. I can only speak my truth and I pray that, by exposing my pain, embarrassments, fears and insecurities, my journey of truth and healing will not be in vain. I hear people say, "Let the past be the past." That may work for some but for me I had to travel back to a dark place. I had to find out why food had become my security blanket, why food became my knight in shining armor.

As a young woman, I would be rich if I counted how many times I heard people say, "You have such a pretty face, if you would just lose weight! Have you ever thought about losing weight or looking like the other kids?" At an early age I started to believe that I was never good enough because I didn't look like the other kids, and from the neck down I was worthless. I carried that through high school and into my adult years.

I had so-called boyfriends who never wanted their friends to see me or never took me on a real date. I was the behind closed doors girl, the one they loved and touched only in darkness. I was the one who would make up fantasy relationships and bragged about my weekends that I really spent alone in front of the TV with pizza and wings. No life and no voice. Alone just me and my comforter, my best friend and companion—FOOD, which was my only means of happiness! I never knew that I was depressed throughout my childhood and adult years. I never knew I was addicted to food because it masked the pain and it was such a comforter. How could it be bad?

If I was angry, alone, afraid, sad, or disappointed it was just a matter of finding the largest meal I could find to soothe my soul. I would be lying if I said it was just sad occasions that I ate. If I was happy, you can best believe I would line up my favorite foods and have a party; with just me, myself, and I. I was an emotional mess! I was on a journey of self-destruction and a road with no destination.

The only happy place for me was the one gift I had of singing. I was popular in school and church because of my singing. I even gave up on that because, again, in my eyes people only heard my voice. They didn't see my face or my pain. I was still the "fat girl," the "failure," and the "sinking ship!"

I began to notice that I was happiest when I was alone with my food and the remote. I would avoid people at all cost. I would lie and say I was sick or had previous plans just to avoid going outside of my comfort zone. If I couldn't get out of it, I would try to arrive first; so I wouldn't be the one that people looked at as I entered the room. I would go to restaurants to make sure I could fit in the seats before everyone else arrived, or I would park and watch everyone go in and then go home, after hitting two or three of my favorite drive thru spots. This behavior was the path to my destruction.

I watched life pass me by as my friends and family were living out their dreams. Listening to their college stories or hearing about engagements, weddings and babies, I was a spectator on the sidelines; watching the joy and laughter of others. For me it was torture! Behind my makeup and outfit (that was way too tight and uncomfortable), behind a fake smile, I was wishing it was my moment, or better yet, thinking of a way to escape these happy people with their perfect lives so I could get back to my —"One True Love"— FOOD!!!

I remember when I met my first so-called boyfriend and I thought I was in love!! What I didn't realize was that he was not interested in me. He was only interested in what he could steal from me, because he was a crack head and a thief!! All I saw was a man paying attention to me. I saw a man who wanted to hold my hand and introduce me to his family. I ignored the missing paychecks and missing jewelry. I ignored his grandmother saying to me, "Child make sure you're ready for this ride." I had no idea she was warning me that I was getting involved with the devil himself. I was so blinded by the fact that I could now tell my friends I had a man. I could go on dates, and I finally had a real story to share about my weekend like my girlfriends. I was now creating my own little love affair no matter how hurtful and mentally abusing it was. I ignored the voices of everyone trying to tell me this was wrong and it wasn't a world I wanted to be a part of.

The cabdriver who said, "Young lady, you're hanging with the wrong one, sweetie. I've known this dude for years and I will take you home free of charge if you promise to leave him alone." Did I listen? NOOOO! I sat my sad tail right there waiting on my so-called man! Talk about a love story gone wrong! The reality was that I knew this man wasn't capable of caring or loving me. The sad part was that I didn't love me enough to get out! I didn't want to face the truth that my pounds and lack of self-esteem supported his HIGH! I was out of control and all I knew was every meal soothed my soul, every meal made me forget him and every meal separated me from the world, one bite at a time!

In 2009, I lost my dad and that was another tragedy for me. To say the least, it was the most devastating time for me and my mom. All of a sudden our lives were literally turned upside down. I just remembered thinking how life can go from smooth sailing to chaos in minutes. I remembered saying to myself, "Chantelle you have to take charge. It's time for you to be the voice and strength that Mommy needs right now." I admit that it was no one but God who walked me through that storm. I also remember looking at the obituary that I put together for my daddy's celebration of life, full of pictures with family and friends, even the dogs, but NOT ONE PICTURE OF ME AND MY DAD!! I was so ashamed of how I looked that I refused to place pictures of me in that obituary. That was another blow to my self-esteem.

Let's jump ahead to the wonderful life of turning 40! I started taking phentermine and getting b12 shots and I felt great! I then tried every shake and any get-thin-quick weight lost scheme that I heard about or saw an infomercial for. I never realized until later that any plan will work for anybody, but not if your mind is still in bondage. I have never admitted to anyone that my highest weight was over 400pds at one point in my life. I never owned a scale because I couldn't weigh on a regular scale. I was at my lowest and I knew I had to get out of this pit or my years would be shortened because of my relationship with FOOD!

I got a promotion at work that involved more than anyone's fair share of traveling, and I must admit I thought to myself, *"This is it. I'm going to lose my job. I can't walk through airports and keep up with everyone else."* I didn't know what would take me out first, the burning in my knees or the burning and shortness of breath in my chest. Again, I felt the pressure of being a failure, so I came up with a plan. I would listen to everyone else's flight plans and choose the opposite. I would arrive to the airport hours ahead of time because I knew I would have to take several breaks while walking to the gate and then the embarrassment of asking for a seatbelt extender and the flight attendant screaming at the top of her lungs, "Ma'am, did you request the extender?" I said, "Yes lady just use the microphone next time why don't you?" (side...eye)

One day, a very dear friend told me about a personal trainer. It was on that day that I wrote an email to a young man who helped change my life. I introduced myself and shared part of my story with a total stranger. I met with him at my home and shared what I wanted to do and how I had to do this, not just for me but for my family and so many others in this RELATIONSHIP... THIS ADDICTION TO AND WITH FOOD!

I started a blog and promised to be honest about my journey. I quickly learned that I could be the best cheerleader for my friends and give the best advice and words of encouragement for everyone but myself. Where was the cheerleader in me? Where was the fight for me? Where was my voice? Where was my love for me? Where was that inner strength that I so boldly bragged about having? Why was I riding this emotional roller coaster again, setting myself up for failure? *I can't do this! I can't fight for me! I'm not worth it! I'll just fail again.* I didn't love me! I didn't love the woman within enough to fight for her. I didn't believe that I was worthy of getting in the ring, and going round after round for me. I was down before I even stepped in the ring. Well, the day my trainer showed up at my door, I had the biggest lump in my throat. I thought of ways to back out and give in. I was talking a good talk but my mind was screaming failure. I said to myself, "You are about to really expose your weaknesses now, Chantelle. You are about to let everyone know that you are worthless and that all you do is give up on you."

Well I met with the personal trainer and he said, "You can do this. You already made the first step and I believe in you. It took a lot of nerve to reach out for help and YOU CAN DO IT!" I stepped out on faith and ignored the voices in my head. I sat in the mirror that night and I apologized to myself for the years of hurt, and the years of not "Loving me from the Inside Out."

The first time I walked up those steps and made it without a burn in my chest was the first time I believed in me. I admit a fire was started within me and I started to see a glimmer of hope. I cleaned out my fridge and my friend said, "It used to look like a bachelor lived here and now it looks like the refrigerator of a WOMAN!" (Side eye…excuse me, sir!)…He almost got that eye dotted (lol) … but I got it … and it changed my view of myself and how I wanted to be seen.

This is a journey of learning to love myself first. This is a journey about a new love! This is my first real relationship. This is a REAL LOVE! This feels so right! This is the first time I have truly learned to LOVE ME FROM THE INSIDE OUT!

We often look at the label on a new garment, to see just how we should care for it. It's important that we get our money's worth and we do what's necessary to keep it in good condition. I didn't care about my old garment and I made sure I followed the label exactly as it read. My old label read, "DON'T HANDLE WITH CARE!" This garment was made with harsh feelings—no love, depressed, a failure, no voice, worthless! Well today my label reads totally differently. Today I'm known as "DESIGNER WEAR!" My new label reads as follows: "Handle with care because she is Priceless!" This garment is made of Self-Love…SHE will never FADE or DECREASE in VALUE! This garment has been washed and cleansed; still covered with flaws but embraced with love and forgiveness. Reversible because she is loved from the Inside—Out!!! I'm finally at a place where I no longer allow myself to label ME with words that can possibly sabotage my journey.

I apologized to the 400 pound young girl that I abandoned and abused for years. I wake up every morning knowing that I am worth having everything God has for me. I have lost 100lbs, and am still fighting this beast one day and one step at a time! I have received more than my share of love and support from my family, friends and my supporters on Facebook! From the depths of my heart, I SAY THANK YOU!

Today I know that I have been forgiven by the abandoned and abused old me. I now protect the new me at all cost. I have forgiven ME and I will never abandon me again. I will never put ME in a box or on a shelf. I'M FINALLY IN LOVE WITH ME! I'M HERE! I'M ALIVE AND I'M FIGHTING! LOVIN ME, EVERYDAY... FROM THE INSIDE.... OUT!

Note to Self: Bad chapters can still be included in a story that ends well. Let your past be part of your story, NOT YOUR IDENTITY!

Dedicated to,

ME

5   _Tragic to Magic: From the Streets to The Pulpit_

Author Andrea Freeman

On November 23, 1972 (Thanksgiving Day), I was born the oldest of my mother's 5 children. My mother was only 17 years old when she had me and within a year and a half, she had a second child from a different man than my father. WOW....18 years old with two children. Although she was very young, I am sure that she never anticipated her life would be so difficult. Well, guess what? IT WAS! I spent my primary school years growing up in a low income project called Washington Park Apartments.

As a young adult, my mother became a victim of domestic violence, which she had to pay a huge price for. It ended in her fatally stabbing my little brother's father, right before his 2-year-old eyes. She began to experiment with drug use, and soon became addicted to them. She was living an absolute nightmare, which led to her own self demise. I and my younger brother just beneath me had to witness all of this.

We were two young children, living in a huge mess. We were on welfare and often faced challenges of living with no food, no lights, constant drug traffic, drug raids, and evictions. It was AWFUL!

Life took a huge turn for my mother, and my brother and I were often left for days at family members' or the home of family friends; while my mother went back and forth to New York and other places. She spent most of my childhood years struggling with drug addiction and in and out of jail. My mother continued having children and things were so bad that we had to be RESCUED. Yes, I said RESCUED, by our grandparents, who I thank God for today. If it had not been for them, I don't know whether or not I would know any of my siblings. I don't even know where I would be.

You may be thinking to yourself, *"Where in the world was your father at when all of this was going on?"* My father was a good dad, or the best dad he knew how to be at the time. He would provide money, clothes, food and necessities as much as he could, but all of that was just not enough. As a child I needed nurturing, a structured home and great role models. Unfortunately, my dad couldn't provide me with that because he was caught up in his own life. His life was unstable, and he was a drinker and a partier. I thank God today for deliverance, because my dad is sober and was delivered from all of that many, many years ago.

Life wasn't an easy journey and, although my parent's talked AT me, they never really took the time to talk TO me. They had their own agendas and they did the best they knew how to, based on their circumstances. That talking AT me didn't help much, because I ended up pregnant in the 8th grade. —"Yes, PREGNANT."— I had my first daughter just as I entered the 9th grade, at 13 years old. My mother fussed and fussed and guess what? It did absolutely NO GOOD because when she finally stopped fussing, I was delivering another baby at 14, entering the 10th grade. Here I am, 14 years old with two babies. Both my daughters were 2 to 2 ½ months premature. I was a mother of what people called the Irish twins, because I had two children within 12 months of each other.

Although I had no clue that I was not on the right path, I did know that I wanted to be a great mother to my children. I wanted my children to have loving parents. I am sure you probably could have guessed that their father went in a separate direction; continuing to have more children around the same time that they were born, and for many years afterwards. All I know is that I looked at them when they were tiny little babies, and made a promise to be the best mommy that I could be. Many people thought that was it for me. People often said, "That girl is going to be just like her mother." Yes, they were exactly right. I am just like her in so many ways, but not in the way they were thinking.

On my 18th birthday, I moved into my own apartment. I was so excited because I was feeling REAL GROWN. I remember my grandmother saying, "You are so happy now but wait until you have to pay rent every month. Wait until you get that light bill. Wait until you get that water bill." I never paid attention to any of it. I thought to myself, *"I am on my own, and I am so happy."*

I was working on the military base at a dining facility, going to cosmetology school, and my dad had co-signed for me a BRAND NEW car (that I couldn't afford). I thought I had it going on. I said, "I am going to prove people wrong because I am never going to do drugs. I will never drink. I will never smoke and I will never leave my babies at other people's homes." I thank God that was a promise that I upheld, but it wasn't long before I had quit my job and become a welfare mother;

living in low income housing just like I grew up in. Yes, I upheld the promise, but it wasn't long before I was selling more drugs than anyone could probably ever imagine. Yes, —"I was."—

I thought I was being so much better than my parents because I was totally against using drugs and alcohol. What I didn't realize was the fact that I was JUST LIKE THEM. I had become a product of my environment. I didn't realize that the cycle had repeated itself. I was caught up in the money. I had a revolving door, and the police were knocking to question a murder that took place a block away. The suspect had just left my home.

In 1992, my house was hot (meaning under police surveillance), and I moved from one city to another. I moved and I thought I was pregnant with my third baby. I found out shortly afterward that I had a molar pregnancy. A molar pregnancy is when an egg with no genetic information is fertilized by a sperm. The sperm grows on its own, but it can only become a lump of tissue. It cannot become a fetus. As this tissue grows, it looks a bit like a cluster of grapes. This cluster of tissue can fill the uterus. The tissue that normally becomes a fetus instead becomes an abnormal growth in your uterus. Even though it isn't an embryo, this growth triggers symptoms of pregnancy. Back then, only one in ten thousand women experienced it.

Although it's not a cancer, it's treated like one. I had to have surgery and chemotherapy to make sure that it didn't come back afterwards. That was a miserable time in my life. The chemotherapy caused me to feel fatigue. I experienced a sore throat, sore gums, loss of all of my hair, and extreme weakness. I had to have regular follow up appointments for one year.

Shortly afterwards, I was pregnant with my third baby girl. Life was life, and nothing had changed, other than having another baby girl. The day she was born, her father missed her birth. He dropped me off at the hospital in labor, and said he was going to get something to eat and come right back. Unfortunately, he never returned. He had been out trying to purchase drugs and had been arrested. I felt like my whole world was upside down. I couldn't wait to be released the next evening so I could figure out how I would get money to get him out of jail.

I went home and later found out that he needed $2,500 to get out of jail. Who in the world had that kind of money? I had $40 to my name on my independence (welfare) card. I called one of his friends and spent my $40 purchasing a small amount of drugs to sell to get him out of jail. With a newborn baby in the house and my older girls asleep, I often stayed outside my apartment building with the baby monitor on my hip, selling drugs. Within one week, I had the money to bail him out. He came home, and I was so happy that he would be able to spend time with his newborn baby.

Several months later— I remember it was on Valentine's Day 1994— the police raided my home looking for him. I happened to be in the kitchen cooking and washing dishes. They hit the door so hard, going straight past the kitchen. I dug in my pocket and put the drugs in the dishwater, and let it out down the sink. As soon as I did that, I remember seeing the red beam of light from an officer's long gun pointing in my face. Thank goodness, he just missed me dispose of what he was looking for.

Several years later, I moved from there to Baltimore. This time, I secretively moved. It was dark outside every time I would move something out. I moved a little here and there. I moved out slowly because I knew that if the police found out I was moving, they were going to kick the door in again before I could get anywhere. Well, I thank God for the move to Baltimore. "Yes, Lord, I thank You." People thought that was the worst move ever, but it ended up being the best. I could only keep driving back to another county just to sell drugs for a limited amount of time. It had become exhausting.

It was summer of 1996, I was pregnant with a 4th baby and things just weren't going as planned. I found out that someone I considered a very close friend let the police in on my little secret, if you know what I mean. They told the police that I had moved and was coming back and forth with drugs. They even had the police follow them to my house one day, while they picked me up to take me back to my old hometown with drugs. They pulled us over just as we crossed into that county and had dogs surrounding us everywhere. I was pregnant and one of my daughters was afraid of dogs, so I had warned her to hang on to me and jump and scream as the dogs approached to sniff me. She did just as she was instructed, fearing that the dogs would bite her and, fortunately, the drugs were not found. They couldn't get the dogs close enough to me because she hung on to me for dear life.

Someone was kind enough to warn me, and when I found out, —"I LET IT ALL GO!"— I quit because I knew where I was on my way to; the same place my mother spent much of her time at— JAIL! Who was going to take care of my kids that I promised to never leave or abandon? That was exactly what I felt my parents had done to me. My grandmother had passed away, and there was NO WAY I could risk losing my babies. I was just tired.

In November of 1996, my mother passed away from AIDS, leaving me to raise my two younger brothers. I thought to myself, *"Now I have 6 kids in my home, what in the world am I going to do?"* Besides, I failed to mention that I had a drug addicted boyfriend who later became my husband. So, in reality, I had a house full of kids. Isn't it funny how I never used drugs but I married an addict? Well, that's because that is what I grew up around and I attracted the same exact type of men that my mother attracted. All I knew how to do was live a lifestyle that revolved around drugs, drugs, drugs.

With trying to raise all of the kids, relying on very small social security and welfare checks, and a husband who could barely keep gas in his car, I had become fed up. I finally realized that I was fortunate enough to have children who went out to school and made honor roll EVERY marking period without my help, while I lay at home and watched soap operas all day. I finally asked myself, "What is it that I want out of life? What am I going to ever be able to teach or even share with my children about the work world if I won't even get up and go to work myself?" The struggle became worse for me and my family.

I started doing hair in the neighborhood and, there were some young girls from a group home who came faithfully. One day, in May of 1998, the director of the group home knocked on my door telling me how much the children loved me and offered me a position. I was so excited. I worked the midnight to 8am shift. I only had to walk directly across the street, about 30 seconds away. The best thing was that I was GETTING PAID. I made big money. I was making $10 an hour. YES, YES! You might think that $10 an hour was nothing, paying full rent with 6 kids, but it was to me.

I had the nerve to have put one of my daughters in Christian school. Not because I wanted any Christian or biblical values imparted to her but because I was too lazy to teach her, so I added another bill. I remember rushing home each day to pick her up from school just to see the Jerry Springer show and she would keep turning the television off. I would threaten her, and she would still turn it off. She would watch me turn on my club music, sing, dance, and clean the kitchen. She would say, "Mommy, is Jesus in your heart or is Satan in your heart? Because Satan is supposed to be under your feet and you act like he is in your heart."

She would tell me how all of her school friends went to church except for her, and she would beg to go. I would often tell her I would go and then back out by saying, I was too tired from work that morning. She was going to school to learn one thing, and would come home to something entirely different. She was 5 years old and desperately seeking a relationship with God. Well, I am so glad that I made the sacrifice to put her in a Christian school setting because God used that little girl to reach me.

I always grew up going to church but I wasn't really saved. My grandparents made me go, so I knew to go. I wasn't living Christ like, and I wasn't even praying. Although I did not honor or even acknowledge Him much, I would have nerve enough to make Him the first person I called in times of trouble.

One evening, I was getting ready to go to work and my mind was wandering all over the place. When I got to work, I waited for all of the other staff to leave, and I decided to do something that I had rarely ever done when I went to work. I turned the television on. As soon as I turned it on, I heard a VERY loud voice and she was shouting. It was Joyce Meyers. I didn't know much about her but had heard of her, and to me it sounded like she was just fussing and fussing, like I always heard my mother and grandmother do. As frustrated as I was feeling on that night, I had finally decided that I didn't want to hear any more of what she was saying. I walked toward the television to turn it off. Just as my finger went to touch the off button, she screamed "DON'T YOU TURN THAT TELEVISION OFF!" I started looking around the room, just in case there was someone in there who I wasn't aware of. I just could not believe it. I was wondering if she could really see me. Everything she was saying related to my circumstances at that given time. I felt like she was talking specifically to me. On that night, that I gave my life to Christ sitting right in front of the television with tears rolling down my face. I said, "I have tried everything else, why not try God?"

It was March of 1999 that I decided to commit to having a GENUINE relationship with Christ, with hopes of improving the quality of my life. I promised Him that if He would just show me a way, I would NOT turn back to the ways of the world, regardless of my temptation. I could not promise to be perfect but I could promise to keep Him first, and I MEANT IT! My relationship with Christ motivated me to keep a job, stay off of welfare, focus on my children getting a great education, and begin furthering my own education.

As my relationship with Christ grew, I began to grow tired of the old and I wanted nothing but the new. I kept telling myself that "old things have passed away; behold, all things have become new." Although I was feeling tired; my level of fear kept me in bondage. I faced evictions month after month, and somehow, God would send that money just before the constable arrived.

My responsibilities and life had been so overwhelming that I became bitter, discouraged, and began losing hope. In silence, I constantly cried and begged to God (with no one else to turn to) to transform me. God said, "Andrea, stop holding on to what's already gone, no more pity parties, you must fight." I couldn't figure out how to fight when I was already tired. God told me to put 'feet' to my faith, and walk it out! He wanted me to stop questioning Him and not to only say I had faith, but to ACTIVATE it.

In 2005, I finally realized that I had to make some painful but necessary decisions, in order to move forward and create a better life and environment for me and my children. I had two brothers who had graduated from high school, two daughters who had gone off to college, two daughters who were attending Christian school at our church, and a failed marriage, which I felt that I had to separate from because my husband had been on drugs throughout our entire relationship. Adultery and other things began to enter the relationship, and I didn't want my daughters to think that those things were acceptable and end up just like I did—attracting the same type of men that my mother did.

In 2008 my oldest two daughters graduated from college and earned their Bachelor of Arts degrees. I knew that it was only through the grace and mercy of God that this happened. I started to feel as if I had really accomplished what had once seemed like the impossible because none of my siblings, first cousins, or their children had graduated from a college at that time. So this was a major accomplishment to me.

Today, not only have all four of my children graduated from high school, but they are all employed and furthering their education. In fact, my oldest daughter recently earned her Master's Degree. I am happy to say that none of my children or younger brothers (that I raised), have ever been in any trouble, and they are all on a path of success.

Through all of that, I said, "I am so tired of my circumstances. My entire life has revolved around parenting, working and paying bills." I thought to myself, *"When does the fun ever come for me?"* In 2008 I started a jewelry and handbag business called Classy Accessories. Not only have I sold my products but I have encouraged people to press forward and start the business of their dreams.

Over time, people started telling me how much I inspired them, saying, "You should be a coach, a counselor, or in leadership in some church."

People even started asking if I could mentor them. Initially, my thoughts were *"Oh no, NOT ME. I am no coach, I am no counselor, I am no mentor, and I don't want any position in any church. NO WAY!"* Some argued, "You are already doing it, because people come to you for advice all the time."

The more I thought about it, the more I wondered if I should start a book club. Immediately God said, "No, not a book club." I said, "Well, what is it, God?" He answered by saying, "Andrea, I want you to start an organization where you will not just inspire or encourage people in your everyday environment, but you will impact lives GLOBALLY!" That was it.

In 2012, I launched a non-profit women's empowerment organization called Changing Lives And Sincerely Supporting You (C.L.A.S.S.Y.), where my vision is to reach and teach women throughout the entire world. About 30 days after launching the organization, God spoke to me and said, "Andrea, the advice you are giving, I want you to start putting it on paper." I immediately started doing so and, 7 short months later, I published my first book. I grew a love and passion for writing and helping others.

I have been consistently taking ministerial courses, and I have been birthed into the prophetic office. I am Prophetess Andrea Freeman and I am teaching and sharing the Word of God on a daily basis. I use my writing as a tool for Christian ministry to help others deepen their love and relationship with God, and to equip them to better serve Him in all that they do. I have a passion for showing the love of Christ to those in need, and believe that all believers should help by being a reflection of the character of our Lord and Savior Jesus Christ.

I believed that I could do something better with my life. As I said in my first book, "I believed that I could create my own future." I wasn't going to sit around and allow my future to be handed down to me. I decided to stop the negative self-talk. I decided to stop saying, "I don't have the resources; I don't have the education," and all of those other FEAR FACTORS that were holding me hostage. I decided to change my mindset and perspective and invite positive thoughts into my life. I had to change my mindset because I realized that my mindset is my GPS! It will direct me wherever I tell it to. I am CHOOSING who I wish to become by creating my own future.

I determined what I needed to do, and what I needed to STOP doing in order to become the person I want to be. I recognized the responsibilities that I needed to take and I stopped minimizing myself. I replaced my toxic behaviors with healthy behaviors to transform my life, and committed to taking RADICAL action immediately. I started feeding my mind a healthy diet and began to think and play big. People have told me that I think too big. My response is, "You think too small."

I was willing to see my brilliance. Are you willing to see yours? You can do everything that I have done, and even more, to get where you want to be. I encourage you to stop doubting your abilities. Stop waiting for validation from others, because you have already been validated by God. You may be struggling, but I promise that if you keep pressing forward and take action, you are destined for greatness. Get up and walk in your God assigned greatness without apology and without regret, because it was no mistake. It was intentional. Start living in the N.O.W. (No Opportunities Wasted), because you are not promised to be here next year. You are not even promised to be here TOMORROW, so you must get up and get moving. If you are feeling broke and broken, you can turn that crawl into a walk, and turn that walk into a run, and turn that run into a soar, so all that you will have to do is keep going, so you can keep soaring.

I know it's hard. Trust me, I do. I am a divorced mother, I am a grandmother, I am a daughter, I am a sister, and I am a friend, just like you. So I know it's hard. Even when you feel discouraged or that your tank is empty, if you can just believe that you can do it, you can. Fuel and ignite your possibilities through belief, hard work, and commitment. Start living by doing what you have to do now, so that you can do what you want to do later. Start planting and sowing seeds on a daily basis so that you can reap your harvest. Keep pressing to create a legacy. Keep pressing to build generational wealth. Keep pressing to impact lives globally, regardless of how long it takes because God wants you to prosper.

You can have all of the insight and education you wish but if you have no action, it's dead weight. There is no big difference between me and anyone else. It was my belief that I could be different that propelled and catapulted me. I believed that I could be a great mom and role model. I believed I could raise kids who would not only be productive in society, but intelligent as well. I BELIEVED. Do you believe? If you do, you must realize that you have to do something different. If you aren't doing anything different, you cannot grow.

I always say that I am so grateful to God for turning my life from TRAGIC TO MAGIC! I am not a genius. I am not a super shero. I am an ordinary woman who chooses everyday super shero behaviors. I am not extraordinary. I am an ordinary woman who chooses to make extraordinary decisions EVERYDAY! It was God's miracle producing power, that CHANGED MY SEASON!

Glory be to God!

Robin Howell Thorne

Ellen M. Johnson

www.ingramcontent.com/pod-product-compliance
Lightning Source LLC
LaVergne TN
LVHW011337080426
835513LV00006B/405